# Australia Wide

This book is dedicated to my five best friends: my saviour Jesus, my wife Pamela, my daughter Jessica, and my Mum and Dad for their example.

I love you all beyond measure.

P A N O G R A P H S ® B Y K E N D U N C A N

Freedom, Seventy Five Mile Beach, Fraser Island, Qld

## Australia Wide

AUSTRALIA WIDE®
FIRST PUBLISHED 2002, REPRINTED 2003 AND 2004.
BY KEN DUNCAN PANOGRAPHS® PTY LIMITED
ABN 21 050 235 606
PO BOX 3015, WAMBERAL NSW 2260, AUSTRALIA.
TELEPHONE: 61 2 4367 6777.
E-MAIL: panos@kenduncan.com

COPYRIGHT PHOTOGRAPHY AND TEXT:
© KEN DUNCAN 2002
PRINTED AND BOUND IN CHINA
THE NATIONAL LIBRARY OF AUSTRALIA
CATALOGUING-IN-PUBLICATION ENTRY:
DUNCAN, KEN.
AUSTRALIA WIDE: THE JOURNEY:PANOGRAPHS.
INCLUDES INDEX.
ISBN 0 9580544 2 8.
1. AUSTRALIA - PICTORIAL WORKS. I. TITLE.
919.400222

**VISIT THE KEN DUNCAN GALLERY ONLINE**
**www.kenduncan.com**

AUSTRALIA WIDE® AND PANOGRAPHS®
ARE REGISTERED TRADEMARKS OF
KEN DUNCAN AUSTRALIA WIDE HOLDINGS PTY LTD.

**Front Cover**
Lagoon Beach, Lord Howe Island, NSW
**Endpapers**
Hangover Bay, Nambung National Park, WA
**Previous Page**
Against All Odds, Silverton, NSW

# Acknowledgments

I would like to offer my sincere thanks to the companies that have supported me in the production of this book.  I have worked with these companies over many years, and know they are strongly committed to Australia.  May they all reap abundantly as they have sown.

Special thanks also to my wife Pamela, my daughter Jessica, all my fantastic staff, my Mum and Dad, Jean McKimmin, Janet Gough, Peter Morley, Peter Friend, Pastors Barry and Lyn Follett, and the many others who have helped either physically or spiritually along the way.  God bless you all.

# Contents

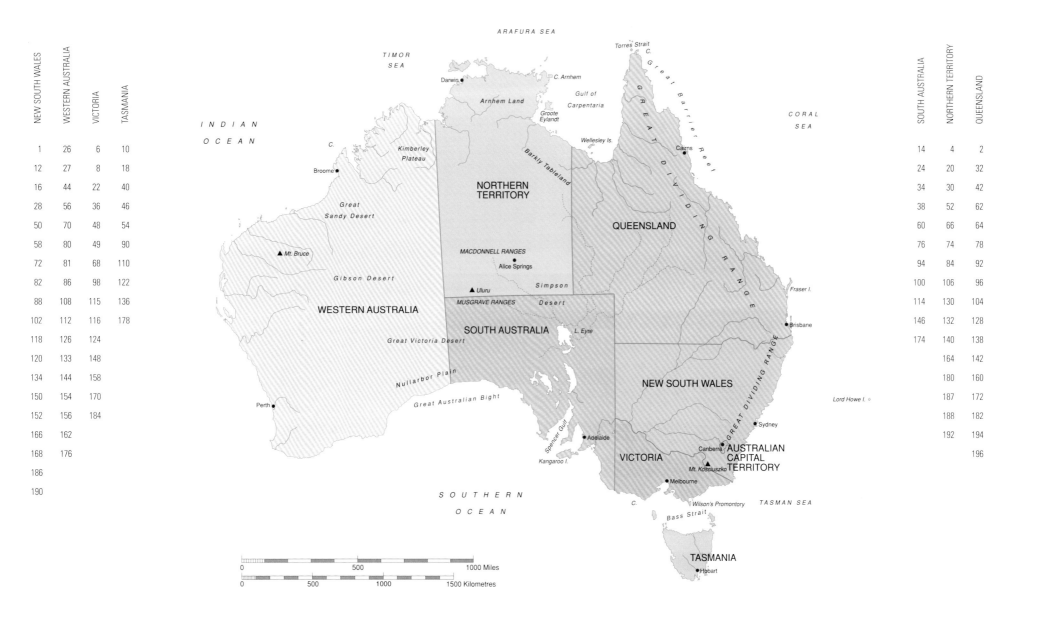

# Introduction

**A** good friend once taught me a valuable lesson. If you really want to get to know a place — as opposed to just being a tourist — you need to spend time in that area. If you really want to get to know a person, you need to 'walk awhile' with that individual. It takes time and understanding to build a relationship. This book is an invitation for you to come 'walk awhile' with me, as I share with you some of my favourite photos – and a few thoughts along the way about my journey through the world's largest island.

I have spent over twenty years roaming this magnificent land, and I have been privileged to get to know a great many true Aussie characters from all sorts of backgrounds. Out in the bush, our so-called civilized classifications mean very little. Country people tend to measure others by their walk, not their talk. Tolerance there is essential, as you often have to rely on those around you. A good sense of humour is also often indispensable. It helps you tolerate different points of view so you can get on with life for the benefit of all.

In the end, regardless of our ethnic, social, religious or political backgrounds, we all share this Great South Land that we call home. It is important therefore that we learn to live together in harmony. The true measure of our character is the love and tolerance we show towards others — and these are far more effective tools for attaining a peaceful society than trying to force our own points of view upon other people. There is a great strength in unity.

I believe the greatest threat Australia faces is not invasion, nor terrorism, but rather the bubbling cauldron of division in our own kitchen, fuelled by intolerance and judgement between various groups.

Once I went sailing around Arnhem Land during the cyclone season. The boat was fairly primitive, the depth sounder our only piece of modern equipment. Our flares were over twelve years old — more dangerous than useful — and we had no radio. There was very little privacy. The only options were above deck, below deck, or off the boat.

There were four of us on that journey and at first everything seemed fine. But it's amazing what comes to the surface when you spend time in close quarters with others. Within days of setting sail, individual attitudes and opinions began to surface. It was an interesting thing to watch. I began to understand how mutiny on the high seas could erupt.

I was determined not to allow the attitudes of others to affect me, and I endeavoured to be the peacemaker wherever possible. But the harder I tried to make peace, the more flack came my way, with each one trying to enlist me on their side to help justify their stance in various arguments. Occasionally I wanted to join in, but I purposed to follow my head rather than my emotions.

We were a divided ship, and consequently our sailing adventure had lost much of its charm! Then one day we ran aground on a sandbank in a very remote area. First came all the recriminations over how we had come to be in such a dangerous situation in crocodile infested waters. The lid was blown off the pressure cooker and steam was being released! But none of the accusations changed the fact that we were stranded together in the middle of nowhere. It was low tide and we were in trouble.

Ultimately, realizing we needed to work together to solve the problem at hand, we combined our individual strengths and were finally able to push the boat off the sandbank. From that moment on, the whole nature of the journey changed. Through adversity we had recognized the need for unity. It was no longer 'me' but 'we'. When we functioned as a team, the journey really became an adventure and we shared some incredible experiences.

I often wonder why it takes adversity to unite people. What a pity we can't just accept that we are all in the same boat together, putting aside our differences to live in harmony with one another. What an adventure we would have if we stopped trying to rock the boat! My dream is that one day Australians will be both unified and tolerant of each other's differences. Perhaps then our light will shine so brightly that others all over the world will see what can be achieved. For in the big picture of Life, we are all in the same boat.

*Ken Duncan.*

Let There Be Joy, Gunnedah, NSW

The Flinders Ranges do not readily yield their natural treasures. To really know this region you have to spend time absorbing its moods until you begin to relate to its mysterious and ancient rhythms. As you humble yourself amid the wonder of creation, the secrets of this distinctive area are granted as gifts in return for your patience. Here, the old, gnarled river gums stand as gateposts alongside the dusty track, beckoning us to enter in and feel the heartbeat of the land.

Lord Howe Island is like a time capsule — a testimony to the way things were years ago, in simpler, more trusting times. Very few establishments offer in-room telephone or television and there is no mobile phone coverage at all on the island. The sense of isolation is fantastic. No one can get to you unless you choose to make contact with the outside world. So the choices are simple: Will I go swimming, fishing, snorkelling, bike riding or walking — or will I just kick back and read a book. To me, this place felt like paradise.

Reach for Life, Russell Falls, Tas

# Forgiveness

rare downfall sends water rushing down the etched sides of Uluru, fresh and pure and white as the tears of God. This photograph is prophetic for our nation. I believe God is grieved by the terrible division between black and white. Here, in the very heart of Australia, we see His pain.

It is tragic how people from different cultures and backgrounds have treated each other throughout Australia's history. Even today the fights go on. In the Bible, God said we would know His people by their fruit – by their actions. The fruit of the Spirit of God is love and joy, peace, patience, kindness, goodness, faithfulness, gentleness and self-control. But the fruit that is most evident in our nation is anger. What can we do to stem the flow of God's tears of grief?

A member of an Australian reconciliation committee once asked me for a comment on reconciliation. I asked for time to pray about it, and as I did the story of a friend came to mind. As a small child she had been abused by her father. Since his death, she had tried to bury the past and get on with her life but the sins committed against her in the past held her captive. She tried all sorts of things to dull the pain of her memories, including drugs, alcohol and other types of destructive behaviour. She sought professional psychiatric help and spent a lot of time sifting through her memories. The doctors encouraged her to hate her father because what he did was wrong. But, as the old rhyme goes, all the king's horses and all the king's men couldn't put Humpty together again. The pain and shame became unbearable and this young lady attempted suicide.

Fortunately, by divine intervention, her life was saved. But the pain continued. This beautiful young woman was snared by the sins of someone in her past — someone who should have known better than to destroy the innocence of a trusting child. What was this woman to do — live the rest of her life as a victim? How could she ever be reconciled to a perpetrator who had passed away?

One night, in desperation, she began to read a Bible. As she read the Lord's prayer she was struck deeply by the words, "Father, forgive us our sins as we forgive those who sin against us." Suddenly a light penetrated the darkness in her heart and she cried out, with the voice of that broken little girl, "Daddy, I forgive you." From that day on a wonderful healing began. Now she is no longer held captive by the past, and through her experience she is able to help lead others out of the darkness of unforgiveness.

The answer to reconciliation, I believe, is this. As grievous as the events of the past may be, we must learn to forgive. While ever we have unforgiveness in our hearts, we bind ourselves to the past. We give victory to the perpetrators of evil, while we hold on to the pain. Now, in Australia, it is time to forgive one another. Forgiveness is the higher road that releases us to soar into those heavenly places where true justice is served.

Southern Dreaming, The Twelve Apostles, Vic

Drifting Sands, Gunyah Beach, SA

A jetty reaches out into the morning mist, like a welcoming hand for all who have dared to venture upon the wondrous seas. Abandoned by the ebb of the massive Kimberley tides, these pearling luggers settle into the mud, their hulls surrounded by protective hessian skirts. The wharf is named after Edwin Streeter, a man of great vision and steel, and an early pioneer of Broome's pearling industry. Time is one of our greatest assets. The way we use it can mean the difference between greatness and mediocrity. Streeter used his time wisely, knowing that time and tide wait for no man.

Although named the 'End of the Line', this is in fact the beginning. The early settlers' port of Cossack in Western Australia, was eventually abandoned by the townspeople when the water supply could no longer support its population. But while the port still operated, this rail line was used to transport supplies to the new inland town of Roeburne. It became a lifeline for Cossack when the old town was no longer capable of sustaining growth. In our own lives too, when problems occur and we find we have run dry, we have two choices. Will we worry about the end, or look forward to a new beginning?

Cedar Falls, Dorrigo National Park, NSW

Peake Ruins, Oodnadatta, SA

Valley Mist, Omeo, Vic

Snug Cove, Kangaroo Island, SA

The Labyrinth, Tas

Imagine, Chilli Beach, QLD

A friend and I had been dropped into this pristine
wilderness by helicopter. Hundreds of kilometres
from the nearest bush track, we swam and drank our
fill of the pure water in the stream above the falls.
That night we made camp under innumerable stars
shining brightly above us, as our campfire crackled in
concert with the flowing stream. Little pockets of
Eden still exist on earth. In the solitude of these
places, amidst the harmony of creation, we feel the
awesome peace of God.

Pine Valley, Cradle Mountain, Lake St.Clair National Park, Tas

Walking into Pine Valley I am awestruck by its mystical splendour — it is like entering the 'Lord of the Rings' movie set. Thick moss forms a spongy carpet and a cool, clear stream meanders along the valley floor. Pandini palms stand by, like characters frozen in time. Scattered throughout the valley, ancient Huon pines — after which the area is named — hulk and tower over the surrounding forest. Some of these trees have been around for over a thousand years. I wonder what these wise old giants think of our cameo parts in the play of life?

Refuge, Wilson's Promontory, Vic

Wangi Falls, Litchfield National Park, NT

Kimberley Boabs, Derby, WA

# Slow Down

Paul Simon sings, "Slow down, you move too fast. Got to make the moment last!" A great thought, but often difficult to achieve. At times we get so caught up in our missions, plans and dreams that it becomes unclear whether we are driving them or vice versa.

Travelling along the Hume Highway, caught up in the flow of the traffic, I almost missed this photograph. But as I glimpsed the old, rustic farmhouse squatting in a brilliant field of flowers, a flicker of potential caught my eye. I felt that with the right light, this scene could work. By the time I was able to stop the car, I had travelled quite a way past the field and wondered if it was really worth the hassle of going back. Perhaps I was just deluding myself. I had other plans — I was heading to a totally different location. I was very tempted to get back onto the highway and keep on driving, but in the end I followed my feelings and headed back to this farm.

The friendly owners gave me permission to camp overnight on their property and photograph the old house at sunrise. They were quite amazed that I would want to shoot the antiquated dwelling they had abandoned years before — which they now expected would simply bow down humbly into the fields. Now they live in a much more practical house in the flat land of the valley. They were delightful people and invited me in for a fantastic country roast dinner, which certainly beat my camp cooking. While we dined together on sumptuous food, they shared some of their memories of the original homestead and helped resurrect the old home in my mind. Maybe this grand old lady had clothed herself in her finest floral garment, just waiting to be immortalized on film.

To me this shot is symbolic of the transience of man's dreams — grand ambitions overtaken by a field of flowers. The lesson I learned in this place is to always be prepared to slow down — even to back up a little — as our expectations may be driving us right on past the blessings that are in store for us. As John Lennon once put it, "Life is what happens while we're busy making other plans."

Fan Palms, Cape Tribulation, Qld

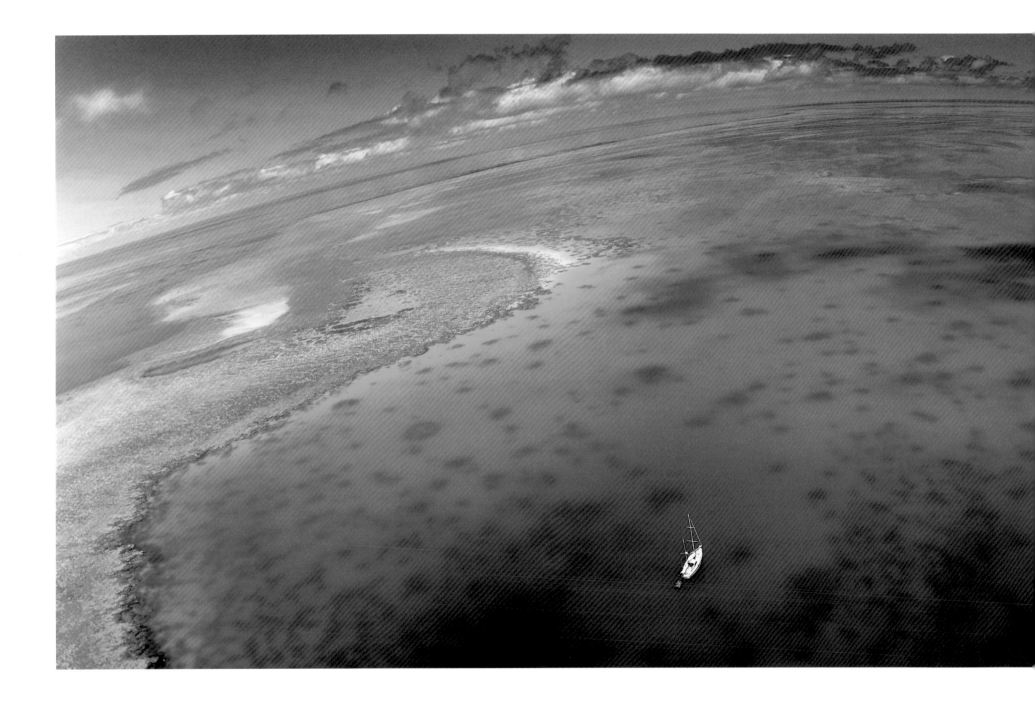

Many share the dream of one day sailing away, and scenes like this make the dream even more appealing. Anchored within Hardys Reef, looking down into crystal clear waters teeming with abundant tropical life – what greater paradise could we imagine! But how many storms has this craft had to weather before this day of glory? How much preparation has it had to endure? Life is full of character building situations, and as we face them we break through to our days of rest.

Shadows creep into the valleys and ravines of Kata Tjuta as darkness approaches and the land prepares for the hush of night. Like Uluru, situated thirty kilometres (18.5 miles) to the east, this extensive maze of domes has been a focus of Aboriginal life and beliefs since ancient times. To stand within its towering amphitheatre is to feel close to the heart of creation. Here, the late afternoon sun glows beneath ominous clouds, illuminating the rich red tones of these magnificent rocks.

Sunset, Kata Tjuta, NT

Dawn of Creation, Mitchell Falls, WA

Secret Falls, Kakadu National Park, NT

The Remarkables, Kangaroo Island, SA

Paradise, Fantome Island, Qld

Divine Motion, Kambalda, WA

Geehi Hut, Kosciuszko National Park, NSW

Heart of a Nation, Uluru, NT

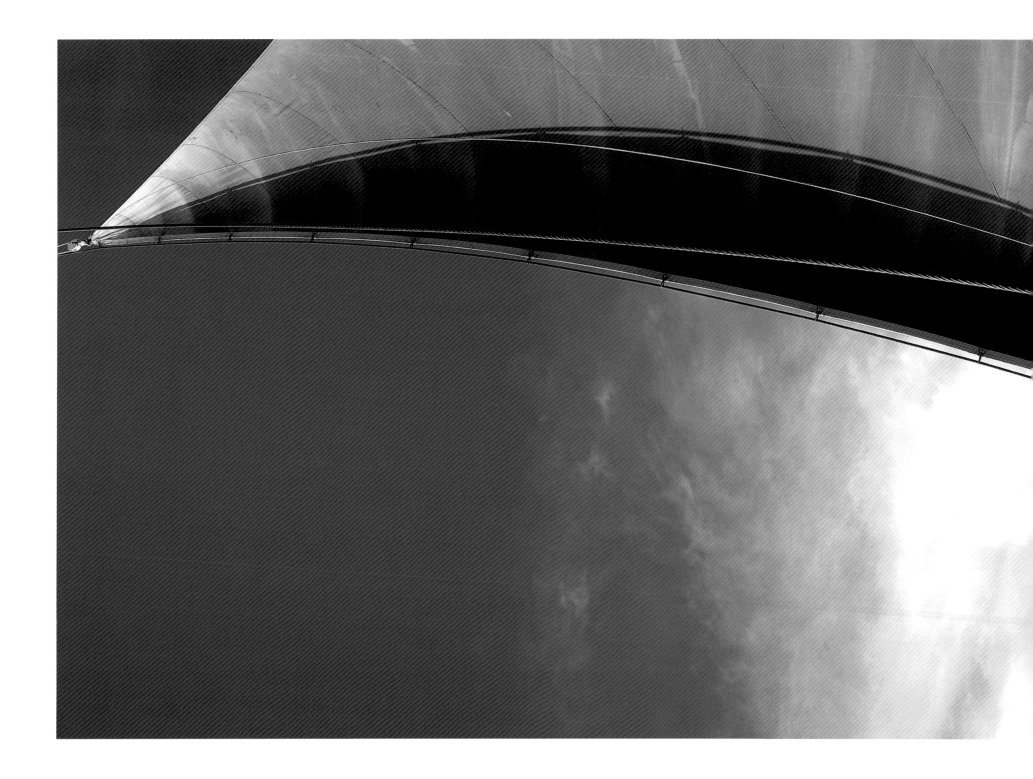

Setting Sail, Pearling Lugger, Broome, WA

There are few things more refreshing or soothing than sitting by a waterfall. Someone once told me that this is because the cascading water increases the oxygen content of the air, making it more invigorating as we breathe it in. Whatever the reason, I love waterfalls and can sit for hours mesmerised by these walls of plummeting water, taking in all the intricacies of the surrounding splendour. The spout on this waterfall made it extra fun to watch and I was severely tempted to slide down the eroded chute. Thank God that common sense prevailed, as the landing certainly doesn't look enticing.

At sunrise we launched our trusty canoe onto the lake in the midst of a dense fog. I had seen these ghostly sentinels the previous day and felt they would look good in the right conditions. We paddled around on the vast lake for hours, virtually shrouded by the thick fog, with no real idea of where we were. Eventually, after much laughter at our plight, the mist suddenly lifted and we found ourselves in precisely the right spot. It reminded me that we don't have to be in control of our own destiny to produce great results.

Winds of Time, Flinders Ranges, SA

Indian Head, Fraser Island, Qld

# Anger or Angels

As I awaited sunrise that morning on North Curl Curl Beach, I had no idea that one of my photographs would reveal in a wave the shape of a huge angel with its wings spread wide. It's harder to see this in the small picture shown, but when seen in a big print the feature becomes obvious. I had arrived well before dawn to get into position before anyone else could spoil my view. Generally, if people realise you were there first, and have been set up waiting for a photo opportunity, they are very understanding and will work around you until you get the shot. I was all set up – just waiting for the sun to rise and light the image that I thought would be a winner.

Suddenly a lady materialized, sat down right in the middle of my shot, and began meditating. She had definitely seen me and must have realised what I was trying to do, but she just ignored me, closed her eyes and began to chant. I would love to say that I felt love for that woman, but my first reaction was annoyance. The only love I could muster at that precise moment was that I would have loved her to move. There she sat, being one with the universe and tuning out everything around her. I called out and asked if she could just move a little to the side for a couple of minutes while I got my picture. Her only reply was to continue her incantation. I was not impressed. After all, I'm part of the universe too. I was tempted to go over and tap her on the shoulder to get her attention, but I knew that would probably have created a conflict situation. So, I started to take it out on God. (He is always listening.) "Hey God, this isn't fair. I was here first." And so on, as if God didn't know what was happening. When I finally ran out of puff, I felt Him say to me, "Ken, just move." So I changed my position.

Within minutes, the sun peeked over the horizon and everything came together in divine timing for this picture to be captured. With all my huffing and puffing I had been so close to missing it. I could have fought for my rights, but ultimately I praised God for the meditating woman. Maybe she was sent to help point me in another direction. If we're not careful, we may get everything our own way and miss the opportunity to be with angels.

Jim Jim Falls, Kakadu, NT

Lucky Bay, Cape Le Grand National Park, WA

Wombat Tarn, Cradle Mountain, Tas

Ochre Cliffs, Cape Lévêque, WA

This 1928 Chevrolet belonged to Bill, a notable Aussie
character and a confirmed bachelor and ladies' man
until the day he died.  He was often seen cruising in
his treasured 'Rattlin' Annie', his name and occupation
proudly displayed on the driver's door.  We found the
car surrounded by chicken wire, choked by weeds and
impossible to photograph.  I asked the property owner,
one of Bill's relatives, if we could move it.  He looked
at me quizzically, but said, "Sure, why not – I've got
nothing better to do."  He hitched the car to his tractor
and helped to reposition it.  After the photo was taken,
Annie was left in this paddock, free once more.

For years this photo existed only in the recesses of my mind. I had been continually on the lookout for a classic shot of a country road threading its way through rolling hills. You would think a shot like this – quintessential Australiana – would be easy to find, but it wasn't. One day while driving into the sun, I was slowly approaching the crest of a hill, not wanting to be surprised by oncoming vehicles. When I glanced into the rear-view mirror, there was the shot I had been searching for. It goes to show that looking back to where we have come from can bring great results. At times we might be in the right place, but looking in the wrong direction.

Rolling Hills, Johanna, Vic

Rising Force, The Skillion, Terrigal, NSW

119

Island Arch, Port Campbell National Park, Vic

Piccaninny Creek, Purnululu National Park, WA

Kakadu Dreaming, NT

As I enjoyed a walkabout with a friend through this
barren area, I was wondering what in the world could
live out here.  Then I saw this scene.  Against all
odds, this Ghost Gum had managed to survive on the
rock face, a living proof of the power of persistence.
This area would be lucky to receive more than a
couple of inches of rain per year.  Yet the tree is firmly
rooted, gaining its sustenance from deep within the
rock.  Possibly the expression "Don't give up the
ghost" was inspired by tenacity such as this.

I first located this arch in the early 1980's when the best way to access The Bungle Bungles (as it was then known) was to be dropped in by helicopter. There was no real road into the area back then – no one was particularly interested in the place – and it was often referred to as 'bad lands'. When people realised the incredible beauty this region had to offer and its obvious tourist potential, suddenly it became very important to various groups. It brings to mind the words of The Eagles' song, "Call some place paradise and kiss it goodbye".

Peace in the Valley, Ebor Falls, NSW

Sunset, Little Henty Beach, Tas

Green Island, Cairns, Qld

Mutitjulu, Water of Life, Uluru, NT

The Mossman River flows from deep within the tropical rainforest, its waters cleansed by the purifying passage. From lofty mountain heights to the hinterland pools below, the waters tumble forth to caress the sandy shores. Boulders, strewn like decorations in the crystal clear ponds, make perfect stools on which to sit and bathe in the beauty of creation. No matter what the heat of day may bring, a plunge into the refreshing waters will cool the body and soothe the soul.

Swimming Hole, Mossman Gorge, Qld

About two hundred kilometres (125 miles) north of Perth, among the extensive sand dunes and scrubby vegetation of the Nambung National Park, the limestone pillars of The Pinnacles rise like phantoms from the barren ground. Standing up to five metres (16 feet) high and moulded by time and weather into varied and often bizarre shapes, they are suggestive of a lunar landscape. They are thought by some scientists to be remnants of ancient forests which once flourished in this area. (The scholars, I suppose, would love to know for sure, but they have never been able to find anyone old enough to verify their theory!)

Squeaky Beach, Wilson's Promontory, Vic

Early Miners Cottage, Hill End, NSW

Craig's Hut, Alpine National Park, Vic

Hinchinbrook Island is a spectacular wilderness of impenetrable jungle, granite mountains, and thick mangrove swamps like those lining the shores of Zoe Creek. Here, where the creek meets the ocean, the languid waters glisten in the sun and the verdant foliage overhangs like a great umbrella, providing a welcome relief from the stinging heat. As the saying goes, "Only mad dogs and Englishmen go out in the noonday sun." But in amongst the mottled shadows you can drowse away the midday hours, or simply relax and contemplate life.

Sheer Majesty, King George Falls, WA

Here I was once again in the middle of nowhere, this time waiting for the midday sun to evenly light both sides of King George Falls. For the past couple of days I had not seen another living soul. Now, just as conditions became perfect, I sighted a small dinghy that had come up river from the coast. Much to my annoyance, it stopped and its occupants began fishing at the base of the falls. I shot the scene anyway, though I felt sure the boat would spoil my photograph. When the dinghy finally left, I got the shot I thought would be a winner. Once again I was wrong! The boat was a miraculous addition that helps give perspective to the falls. I'm sure God gets a laugh at some of my great ideas.

River of Life, Ellery Creek, MacDonnell Ranges, NT

Davistown Jetty, NSW

Lagoon Beach, Lord Howe Island, NSW

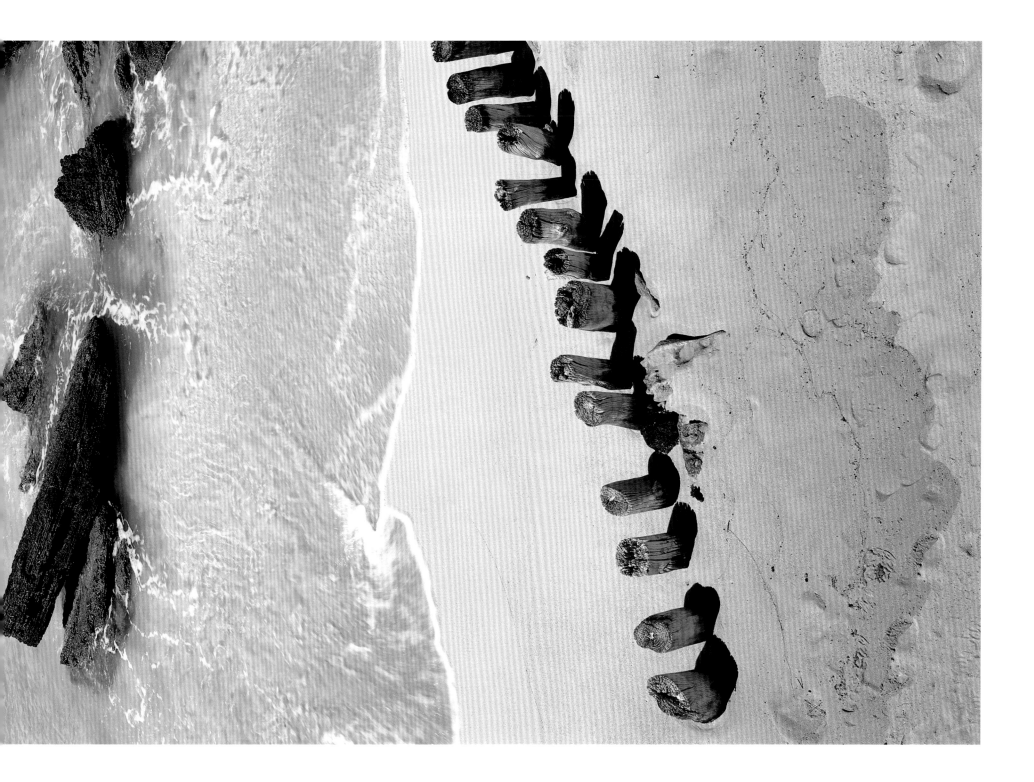

Misty Morning, Strzelecki Ranges, Vic

Crowning Glory, Qld

Ethel Beach, Innes National Park, SA

Sand Dunes, Eucla, WA

Miles and miles of endless sand dunes ripple like a windblown sea. Wandering through the troughs and peaks one can feel like a small rowboat drifting aimlessly in the great expanse.

When I was a young boy I thought cars grew old like people, starting as new models and slowly transforming until they all ended up looking like early T model Fords. In my thinking this would have been a real grand daddy! Fortunately we can transform our thinking as we grow and learn. And if we can change our minds, we can change our lives.

Old Car, Blackmans Bay, Tas

Aerial View, Uluru, NT

Bindari Falls, Vic

Glenworth Valley at Peats Ridge is a magnificent
horse-riding establishment where visitors may ride
unsupervised over thousands of acres of beautiful
pasture. As the fog lifted in the break of early morning
light, the horses hurtled towards the creek in the daily
round up. Balanced precariously on a gatepost as they
galloped up the bank from the creek, I had only one
chance at this shot. As the horses thundered through
the narrow gate, the reverberating power of their
passing almost knocked me from my post.

Uluru has a remarkably humbling presence. Here even the clouds seem to pay homage to the rock as they form a hallowed crown for its head. Creation has the ability to help us keep our dreams and aspirations in perspective – if only we will take the time to look beyond ourselves. Often the only thing blocking the light is our own shadow. But as we gaze upon the beauty of this land, we begin to see the bigger picture, and we realize we all have a part to play.

Sheather's Wharf, Koolewong, NSW

Millstream Falls, Atherton Tableland, Qld

Rainbow Beach, Great Sandy National Park, Qld

# Photographer's Notes

Although people often contact me asking for photographic advice, I do not generally presume to tell anyone how to take photographs. I believe we all see differently and that is what gives each of us our unique style. When we follow our minds we are limited to our own understanding, but when we follow our hearts we see the bigger picture. Having said that, there are a few tips I can pass on.

## BREAK THE RULES

The bottom line is: there are no rules. If an image works, it works; if it doesn't, it doesn't. At one of my exhibitions, a person with a doctorate in photography was looking at one of my shots and I could see she was puzzled. I asked if I could help. "I can't believe this!" she replied. "This guy has the horizon in the middle. It should be one-third sky, two-thirds foreground. But this really works!" The person didn't know I was the photographer, so I simply replied, "Isn't it lucky he doesn't know the rules, or this shot may never have happened."

There's only one essential: make sure you have film in your camera – although I once met a photographer who sometimes left the film out. He wanted to enjoy the privileged position of being a photographer without being disappointed with the results!

## STOP TALKING AND START TAKING

One of the hardest parts of photography is getting out of bed. Just stick a film in your camera and get on with it. If you are going to eat an elephant, the way to do it is one bite at a time. If you sit back and look at how big the elephant is, you'll never finish the 'tusk' at hand! If you have a dream to shoot a book on Australia, you can think of the immensity of the country and be so overwhelmed that you never begin. Or you can pick somewhere to start and attack it one bite at a time. If you persevere, you'll reach your goal.

## LOOKING PAST THE 'I'

Often the biggest thing blocking the light is our own shadow. We can get so locked into what we want to achieve or why we have gone to a particular area that we miss the very thing we are there for.

I believe there is a force at work much bigger than you or I. The key is to tap into the Creator's power rather than your own technical understanding, which by comparison is very limited. This is a hard pill for many to swallow (especially 'techno-heads') because people generally love to be in control. Personally, I would rather be out of control. I'm just an average photographer with a great God.

I have definitely not perfected this area of relinquishing control, but I'm working on it. It's exciting! How small we are and how big He is.

Photo by Gary Johnston

## USING WHAT YOU HAVE

If you are not using what you already have, you won't use what you think you need. Many people think they need a better camera to take photos, and it certainly is nice to have a great camera. But the way to get it is by using the one you have now.

I started taking photos on my Dad's old Praktica, and my first book, *The Last Frontier*, was shot using second-hand Widelux cameras that only cost $250. Talk about equipment with limitations – only three shutter speeds and constant breakdowns – but they did the job. The best understanding of your equipment comes from using it.

The technical aspects of a shot are secondary to capturing the spirit of a moment. Some years ago, at my sister's bidding, I judged a junior school photo competition. Some of the work was good; some was average. But there was one landscape shot which was just awesome. It had been taken at sunset by an 8 year old boy, using a disposable camera through the window of a bus travelling at 100 kilometres per hour! Against all odds, this shot really worked. It certainly humbled me.

## WILD LIGHT

Light is undoubtedly one of the most important things to consider. No light, no photograph! Different light conditions suit different subjects. For example, overcast light may not work for a summer beach shot, but it is great for rainforests, especially during or after light rain.

Early morning and late afternoon is generally the best time to take photographs as the light has great warmth and softness. Uluru in the Northern Territory doesn't actually change colour. It's the changing colour temperature of the light that makes it appear so radiantly red at sunset.

One thing to be careful of is 'blue sky mentality'. Certain parts of Australia are blessed with lots of blue skies and this can sometimes become boring in photographs as the sky often accounts for a large part of an image. Cloudy light or wild, moody light can test your patience but when the break happens, you can get great emotion in a shot. Times of wild light are often when I speak to God asking (respectfully!) such things as, "What are you up to?" or, "Come on, give me a break — please!"

## THE THIRD DIMENSION

Photography is a two dimensional medium, so we sometimes need to create the illusion of a third dimension in our photographs – especially in landscapes – to give depth to the images. A simple way to do this is to use strong foreground interest. Another way is to use lines within the shot to draw the viewer in – a road, a fence, a curve of beach. Sometimes a good way to get better depth in a photo is to shoot from a higher vantage point. I often take shots from the top of my car or standing on my camera case.

## PASSION

Passion is like an artesian well – when tapped, it brings life and energy to even the most barren desert. Passion, like attitude, is contagious and is essential for a project to succeed.

Life is an adventure, not a worry, and if you want to pursue a dream, stumbling blocks must become stepping stones. Passion is a powerful thing and when directed properly it can help bring visions to reality.

## PATIENCE

Photography is like fishing. While you wait, learn the benefit of relaxing and getting into the rhythm of what is happening around you. The fruit that keeps you going is that occasional big catch – a good photo. Patience is a discipline (shocking word) and when we learn to be still, blessings come our way. Once I was shooting in Yosemite National Park and I waited all day for the light to be what I considered 'just right'. Throughout the day, about five other professional-looking photographers came along. Each one pulled out his mega-expensive camera, tripod, the works, waited a couple of minutes, then clicked off a few shots before leaving. Meanwhile, I was still waiting, waiting, waiting - wondering if in fact I had missed something. Finally, right at the end of the day, when all seemed beyond redemption, the light began to dance and the scene came alive. I was the only one still there and I believe I caught the big fish. I hope those others enjoyed their sardines!

For more photo tips, visit my website **www.panographs.com.**

## TECHNICAL ASPECTS

Surround yourself with the best support
Having good suppliers is a key to getting great results. If they are the best in their fields then you won't have to worry about that aspect of your photography. Here are some contacts I highly recommend for various services.

### For Photographic Printing

CFL Print Studio in Australia is the best digital Ilfochrome (Cibachrome) print lab I have found anywhere. (Telephone: +61 2 4365 1488 or Email: info@cfl.com)

### Airline Travel

There is no better Airline company than Qantas. I have spent hundreds of hours flying with them shooting for various projects all over the world. They are fantastic.

### Courier Services

There is no international air express company that surpasses FedEx. Their parcel tracking system is phenomenal and their speed and reliability are legendary.

### The equipment I use

• My main camera is a Linhof 617 III S with three interchangeable lenses – 180mm, 90mm and 72mm. It uses 120 roll film and gives 4 shots to a roll with an image size of 6cm x 17cm. I believe this is the best medium-format panoramic camera on the market.
• I use a Manfrotto carbon fibre tripod with ball head and quick-release mounts. Nearly all my images are shot from a tripod and this one is light and quick to set up, which helps with urgent shots.
• I also use Noblex cameras, both Pro 6/150U (120mm roll film) and a 135U (35mm roll film). These are my pick of the rotating lens cameras as they have great depth of field and are easily hand held.
• For light readings I use a Sekonic spot meter as well as my trusty Nikon F90X which also allows me to grab some 35mm shots along the way.
• I use Hi-Tec filters – specifically an 81B colour correction filter (but not at sunrise or sunset) and occasionally a graduated neutral density filter to hold back the skies. I also sometimes use a graduated, slightly warming filter to help with the colour on those really dull days. However, I use natural light wherever possible.
• My film of choice is Fuji – it's the only film able to capture the amazing diversity of Australia's light and colour. I mainly use Velvia.

### Ken Duncan Online Gallery

For information on Limited Edition Prints from this book, and to see other products, visit our website: **www.kenduncan.com**

# Index